BEST FRIENDS FOREVER!

And More True Stories of Animal Friendships

Published by the National Geographic Society
John M. Fahey, *Chairman of the Board and Chief Executive Officer*
Declan Moore, *Executive Vice President; President, Publishing and Travel*
Melina Gerosa Bellows, *Executive Vice President; Chief Creative Officer, Books, Kids, and Family*

Prepared by the Book Division
Hector Sierra, *Senior Vice President and General Manager*
Nancy Laties Feresten, *Senior Vice President, Kids Publishing and Media*
Jonathan Halling, *Design Director, Books and Children's Publishing*
Jay Sumner, *Director of Photography, Children's Publishing*
Jennifer Emmett, *Vice President, Editorial Director, Children's Books*
Eva Absher-Schantz, *Design Director, Kids Publishing and Media*
R. Gary Colbert, *Production Director*
Jennifer A. Thornton, *Director of Managing Editorial*

Staff for This Book
Marfé Ferguson Delano, *Project Editor*
Becky Baines, *Editor*
Lisa Jewell, *Illustrations Editor*
David Seager, *Art Director*
Ruthie Thompson, *Designer*
Grace Hill and Michael O'Connor, *Associate Managing Editors*
Joan Gossett, *Production Editor*
Lewis R. Bassford, *Production Manager*
Susan Borke, *Legal and Business Affairs*
Ariane Szu-Tu, *Editorial Assistant*
Callie Broaddus, *Design Production Assistant*
Hillary Moloney, *Illustrations Assistant*

Manufacturing and Quality Management
Phillip L. Schlosser, *Senior Vice President*
Chris Brown, *Vice President, NG Book Manufacturing*
George Bounelis, *Vice President, Production Services*
Nicole Elliott, *Manager*
Rachel Faulise, *Manager*
Robert L. Barr, *Manager*

The National Geographic Society is one of the world's largest nonprofit scientific and educational organizations. Founded in 1888 to "increase and diffuse geographic knowledge," the Society's mission is to inspire people to care about the planet. It reaches more than 400 million people worldwide each month through its official journal, *National Geographic,* and other magazines; National Geographic Channel; television documentaries; music; radio; films; books; DVDs; maps; exhibitions; live events; school publishing programs; interactive media; and merchandise. National Geographic has funded more than 10,000 scientific research, conservation, and exploration projects and supports an education program promoting geographic literacy.

For more information, please visit www.nationalgeographic.com, call 1-800-NGS LINE (647-5463), or write to the following address:
National Geographic Society
1145 17th Street N.W.
Washington, D.C. 20036-4688 U.S.A.

Visit us online at www.nationalgeographic.com/books

For librarians and teachers: www.ngchildrensbooks.org

More for kids from National Geographic: kids.nationalgeographic.com

For information about special discounts for bulk purchases, please contact National Geographic Books Special Sales: ngspecsales@ngs.org

For rights or permissions inquiries, please contact National Geographic Books Subsidiary Rights: ngbookrights@ngs.org

Trade paperback
ISBN: 978-1-4263-0935-9
Reinforced library edition
ISBN: 978-1-4263-0954-0

Printed in China
13/RRDS/1

Table of CONTENTS

ROSCOE AND SURYIA: BEST FRIENDS FOREVER

It was love at first sight when Suryia the orangutan met this dog named Roscoe.

Bubbles gives a lift to Suryia, Roscoe, and animal trainer Moksha Bybee.

Chapter 1

The BEST DAY Ever

**Summer 2008,
Myrtle Beach, South Carolina**

It was a muggy, hot day. An elephant named Bubbles strolled through the woods. On her back bounced a fuzzy-haired orangutan named Suryia (sounds like SUR-ee-uh). Bubbles and Suryia were excited. They knew there was a river at the end of the path. Soon they were going to be *in* that river. They were going for a swim!

A man named Doc walked beside Bubbles and Suryia. Looking ahead, he saw a hound dog. It sat alone on the riverbank. It looked like a hungry dog. It was so skinny you could see its ribs. Just then, Suryia spied the dog, too. Before Doc could stop him, the playful ape jumped off Bubbles.

Suryia ran to the dog. He threw his long, hairy arms around it. *Uh-oh,* thought Doc. *A hungry dog might be a mean dog.*

But the dog didn't mind a big, hairy hug. He even wagged his tail. Then he pounced at Suryia. The seven-year-old orangutan pounced back. That was their I-like-you, do-you-like-me? moment. The answer was yes!

The new pals chased each other in circles. Then they flopped down to rest. The orangutan put his arm around the dog. He pulled him close. They acted "like long lost friends," Doc said.

After a while it was time to leave. Doc lifted Suryia back onto Bubbles. He tried to send the dog back to its own home.

But the dog followed them. He wagged his tail all the way. Wherever Suryia was, that's where the dog wanted to be. "I guess you've decided to stay," said Doc. He named the dog Roscoe.

Doc is Dr. Bhagavan Antle (sounds like BAG-uh-vahn ANN-tuhl). He is the director of a wildlife preserve in Myrtle Beach, South Carolina. Suryia and Bubbles are just two of the animals that live there.

Doc and the other caregivers at the preserve also look after lions and tigers. They care for leopards and cheetahs. They watch over monkeys, chimpanzees, and other orangutans like Suryia. There's even a liger (sounds like LIE-ger) named Hercules at the preserve. A liger is the cub of a lion father and a tiger mother.

Now Doc had a new animal to take care of, and Suryia had a new best friend.

Roscoe is a bluetick coonhound. Blueticks are smart and friendly. They really like to hunt. Blueticks keep their noses to the ground, sniffing for clues. They forget everything except *Find it, find it!*

Island Homes

Orangutans used to live everywhere in Asia. Today they live in the wild on only two small islands. These are Sumatra (sounds like sue-MAH-tra) and Borneo (sounds like BORE-nee-oh).

Wild orangutans make their homes in rain forests. Farmers and loggers are cutting down the forests on these islands. They want to make palm tree farms. This leaves orangutans with even fewer places to live. It is harder for them to find food. Unless their forest homes are protected, there will soon be no more wild orangutans.

A bluetick coonhound won't stop until it catches its prey or chases it up a tree.

Roscoe might have been hunting the day he met Suryia. Maybe he went too far. Maybe he could not find his way back home. Maybe he did not have a home.

At first, Doc kept a careful eye on Suryia and Roscoe. Animals often get scared when something new enters their world. Suryia had never been face-to-face with a dog before. Had Roscoe ever met an orangutan? Not likely!

Scared dogs growl. They show their teeth. Their ears go back. The hair on their back stands straight up. When orangutans get scared, they look like they're smiling. A silly grin on their face means they're shaking inside. Doc never saw anything like that on Suryia's face. And Roscoe never growled. He never showed other signs of fear, either. Not even once.

Since the day they met, it's been Suryia and Roscoe, best friends forever. Neither one is the boss. If Roscoe wants to nap, Suryia flops down beside him. If Suryia lies down to rest, Roscoe does, too.

Suryia is better at sharing than Roscoe, however. Suryia shares everything. He breaks up his cookies and feeds pieces to Roscoe. Roscoe really likes Suryia's special monkey cookies.

Suryia also tries to share bananas with Roscoe. Roscoe does *not* like bananas. He will not open his mouth. He turns his face away. Then Suryia gives up. He eats the banana himself. Suryia loves bananas.

Best buds since the day they met, Suryia and Roscoe enjoy cuddling up with each other.

Chapter 2

Ambassador SURYIA

Suryia has a special job at the animal preserve. He is one of Doc's "animal ambassadors" (sounds like am-BASS-uh-ders). The word "ambassador" usually means a person who represents his or her country. Suryia's job is to represent orangutans that live in the rain forests.

Doc thinks it's good for people to see Suryia and the other animals at the preserve up close. He wants people to see them in action. He hopes this will make people want to help protect the animals' relatives in the wild.

Suryia is a great animal ambassador. People just love to watch him. When Suryia and Roscoe are together, they really draw a crowd!

Sometimes the two friends walk in the yard together. Suryia grabs Roscoe's leash and tugs it. That gets his pal going. They stroll around for a few minutes. Soon Suryia does more than just walk. He grabs his feet and rounds himself into a ball. Over and over he rolls. He falls on Roscoe. Then Roscoe jumps on top of him. Suryia pulls the leash one way. Roscoe tugs it back the other way. There is no such thing as walking in a straight line for these two.

Suryia can have fun with almost anything. For him, an empty box is a fine place to sit. Then he puts the box on his head like a hat. It gets a little ripped. That makes it into a good superhero cape! Soon the box is completely torn open. Now Suryia crawls under it. Does anyone want to play hide-and-seek?

Like all orangutans, Suryia likes to make faces. He pulls his bottom lip out. He puckers his rubbery lips. He makes silly smiles. He sticks out his tongue. He wipes his face down with his hand and plays peek-a-boo. Sometimes he blows *pfffffft* sounds. That always makes people laugh.

People don't get tired of watching Suryia. But Suryia does get tired of watching people. He would rather play with Roscoe. He likes to hang out with other orangutans, too.

Lucky Suryia! One of his other jobs is doing exactly that—hanging out with other orangutans. Or really, to let them hang out with him. In the wild, baby orangutans learn about life from their families. At they preserve, they learn from Suryia. They learn by watching and playing with him.

If Suryia lived in the wild, he'd be on his own by now. At the preserve he lives in a house with three younger orangutans. An animal trainer named Moksha Bybee (sounds like MOKE-shuh BYE-bee) lives with them.

Suryia and the three little orangutans love to wrestle. They have fun tickling each other. They run and roll across the yard. Sometimes Suryia grabs a twig to scratch his back. The little ones find their own twigs. They try to scratch their backs. Sometimes Suryia makes kiss-kiss noises at the babies. They make kiss-kiss noises back.

Most of the time Suryia gets along just fine with the little orangutans. But at mealtimes he has to eat by himself. Otherwise, Suryia would grab their food. That's just what older orangutans do.

In the evening, Moksha gives the orangutans a bath. She puts them in the tub. She tries to wash them. They just want to splash. They want to play. This surprises Moksha. In the wild, orangutans do not like water. In the wild, water means danger. In the tub, water means fun.

Lots of things would be different for Suryia if he lived in the wild. At the preserve, he spends his days with lots of other animals. In the rain forest, he would spend his days alone. He would look for food alone. At night he would make a nest of leaves in a treetop and sleep alone. He would not have a dog as a friend!

At the preserve, Moksha helps the young orangutans get ready for bedtime. She pulls blankets into round, soft nests for them. Suryia makes his blanket nest all by himself.

Before lights out, Moksha does one more thing. She calls, "Roscoe, bedtime!" Roscoe runs into the house. Then he curls up to sleep next to his best friend, Suryia.

Orangutan School

In Sumatra and Borneo, wildlife workers run special schools for young orangutans that don't have moms. The workers teach them skills they need to survive in the wild.

Wild orangutans live in trees. They can go for weeks without touching the ground. At orangutan school, baby orangutans practice on jungle gyms made of ropes and netting. They learn how to climb up and stay up. If a baby goes too high and gets scared, a worker helps it back down. After a cuddle, it's time for another try!

Suryia hitches a ride around the pool from Roscoe. The dog doesn't mind, and Suryia loves it!

SWIM Buddies

Nothing beats a swim on a hot summer's day, right? How about going swimming with your best friend? Even better!

Orangutans are not natural-born swimmers. Rivers in their jungle homes can be dangerous places. If a river is flowing fast, an orangutan that falls in might get swept away.

But Suryia doesn't live in the wild. And Moksha knew how much

Suryia loved being in the bathtub. *Hmmm,* thought Moksha. *I wonder if Suryia would like to learn how to swim?*

When Moksha told Doc her idea, he told her to give it a try. So, one day she strapped a life vest on Suryia. She took him to one of the pools on the preserve. It was time for a swimming lesson.

Into the water they went. At first Suryia clung to the side of the pool. He curled the fingers of one hand tightly over the edge. Moksha stood in the water a few steps away from him.

"Come on, Suryia!" she shouted. "Swim to me!" Suryia reached out to Moksha. Looking at her, he let go of the edge. His long arms stretched out and pulled him through the water. Suryia was swimming!

Now Suryia loves to swim. He still needs a life vest. That's because he doesn't quite understand how to cup his hands. So it's hard to get a good pull. Plus, orangutans have very solid, or dense (sounds like DENTS), bodies. That makes it nearly impossible for them to float.

Like many hunting dogs, Roscoe is a great swimmer. Sometimes Suryia holds Roscoe's tail and gets a ride around the pool. *Whee!*

When Moksha taught Suryia to swim, she watched him very closely to see how he was feeling. His body language helps him communicate.

Swinging Swimmers

In 2009, some orangutans in Borneo did something very surprising. They took a swim. They dropped into the river from branches above. They splashed around. It was like a pool party! Scientists were amazed. No one had ever seen a wild orangutan swim before. The story made the news around the world.

The orangutans were at a rescue center. Scientists think they felt safe. They may have noticed there were no crocodiles in the area. The orangutans searched for food in the water. They also ate fish. And they drank from cup-shaped rocks. Amazing!

If Suryia pulls his lips back to show his teeth, that means he's feeling scared or angry. Moksha saw that look once or twice at the start of the swim lessons. When he opens his mouth but doesn't show any teeth, he's ready to play. A sideways look says, "Calm down. Stop moving." Roscoe gets that sideways look a lot from Suryia.

Doc, Suryia, and Bubbles still go down to the river to swim. Only now, Roscoe rides on top of Bubbles with Suryia. When they head for the path through the woods, both Suryia and Roscoe get excited. They know where they're going! Suryia claps his hands, and Roscoe lets loose with a howl. *Aaah-roooo! How great is this?* he seems to say. *I'm going swimming with my best friend ever!*

Ever since she was a baby, Koko the gorilla has loved cats. Here, she is with Tiger.

KOKO: CRAZY FOR CATS!

Koko is not just big, she is beautiful! She is also smart and loving. You can see it in her eyes.

Chapter 1

Worst Present EVER

December 1983, Woodside, California

It was Christmas morning. Twelve-year-old Koko had presents to open. First the gorilla looked in her stocking. She found some nuts in it. Koko loved nuts. But this morning, she tossed them aside. Then she unwrapped a doll. "That stink," she told her friend Penny.

Next came a toy cat made of cement. It was covered with black velvet. "That *red!*" Koko exclaimed. Red is not a good thing. When Koko uses the word "red" like that, it means she's angry.

Uh-oh. Penny knew Koko wanted a cat. She bought one that could stand up to rough gorilla play. She thought the cement cat was a good present. Koko let Penny know she was wrong. Penny understood. *Koko wants a* real *cat.*

Wait a minute—how could a gorilla tell a human how she felt?

Koko isn't just any gorilla. She's an *amazing* gorilla. She can communicate with American Sign Language, called ASL for short.

ASL is not a spoken language. With ASL you make words with your hands, face, and body. Many people who cannot hear use ASL to speak without sound.

Imagine you are with Koko right now. If you knew ASL you could ask her, "Who are you?" She might sign back, "Fine person gorilla me."

How did Koko learn sign language? Around the time Koko was born, Penny Patterson was a student at Stanford University. She heard scientists Allen and Beatrix Gardner speak about an amazing project. They had taught ASL to a chimpanzee named Washoe (sounds like WASH-oh). Washoe was the first non-human ever to learn how to use ASL. She learned 350 signs.

Koko's Special Signs

People around the world use different kinds of sign language. In China, people use Chinese Sign Language. They would not understand American Sign Language. And people who use ASL may not understand Gorilla Sign Language.

Koko has smaller thumbs than a human does. This means she can't make some ASL signs. So Koko makes up her own signs. She signs "zebra" as "white tiger." A mask is "eye hat." A ring is "finger bracelet." Koko can be very creative!

Penny decided she wanted to teach an ape to communicate with ASL. Maybe she could find a chimpanzee to teach.

As it turns out, she got a gorilla— Koko! Gorillas and chimpanzees are both in the Great Ape family. They are alike in many ways. Both are very smart.

Koko was born at the San Francisco Zoo on July 4, 1971. When Koko was a year old, Penny talked with the director of the zoo. She asked if she could teach Koko. Penny promised to stay with Koko for four years.

Guess how long Penny stayed with Koko? It's been more than 40 years now! Penny is still Koko's friend and teacher. But now Penny gives better presents. The next present she gave Koko was much better.

Koko cuddles All Ball, her first real kitten. Koko loved to stroke All Ball's head with her finger.

Chapter 2

A KITTEN TO LOVE

A few months after that disappointing Christmas, Penny decided to get Koko a real cat. She was as sure as she could be that Koko would not hurt a kitten. After all, Koko loved cats. Her favorite stories were "Puss in Boots" and "The Three Little Kittens."

One day Penny heard about three kittens that had lost their

mother. Penny had them brought to the Gorilla Foundation, in Woodside, California. She and Koko live there in side-by-side houses.

Penny took the kittens to meet Koko. One was brown, and two were gray. One of the gray ones had no tail. Koko signed, "Love that," when she saw the kittens.

Penny told Koko she could choose one kitten. Koko picked them up one by one. She looked in their eyes. She blew in their faces. She does this when she meets a new animal or person. Then she chose the gray kitten with no tail. "Koko love," she signed.

"What will you name the kitty?" Penny asked.

"All Ball," Koko signed. With no tail, it really did look like a ball of soft gray fur.

Koko tucked All Ball's tiny gray head against her big furry belly. She was very gentle with All Ball. She treated him like a baby. A gorilla baby. Koko pushed All Ball up on her back. Mother gorillas carry their babies on their backs.

All Ball climbed all over Koko. Sometimes the little kitten used his sharp claws to climb. *Ouch!* Koko signed, "Cat do scratch."

All Ball turned out to be a little rowdy. It might be because he was orphaned when he was still young. He had no mother to teach him to be gentle. Sometimes All Ball bit Koko. "Cat bite. Obnoxious," Koko signed. Did Koko ever scratch or bite back? Nope. She was patient with her new little friend.

Koko liked to groom All Ball. She combed his hair. She petted him. Every day she looked carefully into his eyes, ears, and mouth to make sure everything was all right. What a good friend!

Koko liked to talk about All Ball. She had many conversations with Barbara Hiller. Barbara was a co-founder with Penny of the Gorilla Foundation. When Barbara asked Koko to tell about All Ball she signed, "Soft."

"Do you love All Ball?" Barbara asked.

"Soft good cat cat," signed Koko.

Koko loving All Ball? No problem. Koko playing with him? That could be a *big* problem. At the time, Koko weighed

200 pounds (91 kg) and stood 5 feet (152 cm) tall. All Ball weighed 6 ounces (.17 kg) and was 4 inches (10 cm) tall. That's like you playing with a butterfly. When Koko and All Ball were lying on the floor, Koko would sign, "Tickle." Koko loves being tickled. If All Ball knew what "tickle" meant, he would have said, "No way!" All Ball did *not* like to be tickled.

So Penny helped Koko pretend that All Ball was playing tickle. Penny held All Ball in one hand and tickled Koko with the other. That worked. Koko thought this was a funny idea. "Huh, huh, huh," laughed Koko, as she pretended to be tickled by her pal.

Another favorite Koko game is chase. Can you imagine a game of chase between a gorilla and a kitten? Cats like to be the chaser. So does Koko. Koko tried to chase All Ball. But the kitten stood still and arched his back. That was OK with Koko. Nothing about All Ball made Koko mad or sad.

Then one day something awful happened. All Ball slipped out the door. He ran into the road, and a car hit him.

Penny told Koko about the accident. Koko did not say anything. At first Penny thought she did not understand. But when she closed the door to Koko's home, she heard Koko start to hoot, soft and sad. Penny cried, too. Koko was crying for her friend All Ball. Penny was crying for All Ball and Koko.

Gentle Giants

There are two kinds of gorillas. Mountain gorillas live in forests in the eastern part of Africa. Lowland gorillas roam forests in western Africa. Koko is a lowland gorilla. Free-living gorillas chow down on wild celery and roots. They munch on fruit and bamboo shoots. They also eat tree bark and pulp.

Gorillas may look a little scary. But most of the time they are gentle and peaceful. They share their food. They protect their babies. They can feel happy or sad. Just like humans.

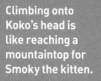
Climbing onto Koko's head is like reaching a mountaintop for Smoky the kitten.

SORRY, Koko Love Good

Three days went by before Penny asked Koko about All Ball. She asked, "Do you want to talk about your kitty?" Koko signed, "Cry." Then she signed, "Want."

Penny asked if Koko could say what happened. Koko signed, "Sleep cat." Penny asked how Koko felt. Koko signed, "Bad, sorry, Koko love good."

Another time Koko saw a picture of a kitten that looked a lot like All Ball. She pointed to the picture and signed, "Cry, sad, frown." She put her finger to her eye to show the path of a tear. She pulled her bottom lip down to sign "frown." This was a very sad time for Koko. It hurts to lose someone you love.

Penny decided to get a new kitten for Koko. She found a family with a kitten to share. They brought it to Koko in a box.

What? Only one kitten? Koko pointed to the box. She signed, "Pick there."

Koko wanted to choose her own cat. Now she got grumpy. "Think fake look," she signed to Penny. She didn't get to see two or three kittens rolling around. It *was* a fake look!

The new kitten was orange with a bright pink nose. Koko named him Lips Lipstick. Penny thinks its pink nose made Koko think of lipstick. Koko played with Lips, but she just didn't seem to love this kitty the way she loved All Ball. Somebody else did, though.

Michael was another gorilla at the Gorilla Foundation. He was also learning sign language from Penny and other staff members. It's a good thing Koko had Michael as a playmate. When a gorilla wants to have wild crazy fun, only another gorilla can keep up! These two romped like brother and sister.

Just like a brother and sister, if Koko had a cat, Michael wanted a cat. He called Lips "my cat red." Since Michael seemed

Did You Know?

A group of gorillas
is called a troop.

to care more about Lips
than Koko did, Penny
gave the kitty to him.

For her next kitten, Koko had a choice.
Penny brought her two kittens. One was
black and white. Koko petted it first. But
when she lifted it out of the box, it ran
away. Koko caught the kitten. Then she
signed, "Baby, baby, baby obnoxious, darn."

The other kitten was gray. This one ran
right into Koko's lap. Koko said, "Mine
Koko love." Koko kissed the kitty and
walked a few steps away. The kitten
followed her. "Love," signed Koko,
cradling the kitten. Then she showed the
kitten her favorite doll. Koko placed a
bead necklace around the kitten's neck.
This one was a keeper.

A few days later Penny asked Koko if she had named her new friend yet. "That smoke," said Koko. And Smoky was its name.

Over the years, other cats have come to live at the Gorilla Foundation. But these days Koko has a new interest: babies. Not human babies, gorilla babies. She has a special gorilla friend named Ndume (sounds like en-DOO-may). Ndume is male. Penny and the other scientists at the Gorilla Foundation hope Koko and Ndume will have babies together.

If Koko does have a baby, will she teach it to sign? Penny thinks she might. When Koko plays with her dolls, she moves their arms and pretends they are signing. Maybe she's just practicing until she has a real, live baby to teach.

Naughty Name Callers

Just like humans, Michael and Koko found it hard to be on their best behavior all the time. One time Michael misbehaved. Penny had to scold him and remind him to be a good gorilla. She could hear Koko making a "huh, huh, huh" sound. Koko thought it was funny that Michael got in trouble.

Another time Michael and Koko called each other names. Koko called Michael "Stupid toilet." Michael called Koko "Stink bad squash gorilla." Those were big naughty words, and they both knew it!

In the meantime, Koko has plenty to keep her busy. She works with Penny and plays with Ndume. She uses more than 1,000 ASL signs. She enjoys drinking tea and looking at magazines. She also teaches Penny and other Gorilla Foundation scientists something new every day.

In November 2011, Koko picked two new friends from a litter of kittens. One had stripes like a tiger. The other was all black. What do you think Koko named them? Tiger and Blackie! Koko is a good friend to them. She tucks them in her nest of blankets. She boosts them up on her shoulders. She cradles them in her arms. Clever Koko picked two kittens who like being friends with a gorilla. Koko is still crazy for cats!

JASMINE: SUPER-FRIEND!

Jasmine the greyhound snuggles with some of her friends. Which one thinks she's a *hoot* to play with?

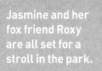
Jasmine and her fox friend Roxy are all set for a stroll in the park.

LEARNING TO TRUST

Nuneaton, England, 2003

Inside a dark garden shed, a young dog whimpered. She was all alone. She was very hungry and very scared. Someone had locked her in the shed and just left her there. Day after day passed. No one came to feed her or check on her. She grew weaker and weaker.

It's a good thing some police officers found the dog before it was too late. They could tell she needed special care to get better. So they took the dog to a person named Geoff (sounds like JEFF) Grewcock.

Geoff lives in England in a town called Nuneaton (sounds like nun-EE-ton). He has a soft spot in his heart for every animal in need. In 2001 he set up an animal sanctuary (sounds like SANK-choo-air-ee) in his own home to help them. It's a place where he and other volunteers care for animals that are sick or hurt or have lost their mothers. Once the animals can survive on their own, they are released back into the wild.

The dog the police brought to Geoff was not a wild animal. But she sure needed help. Her eyes were dull. Her skin lay on her ribs like a thin blanket. As soon as Geoff saw her, he knew he had to help her.

Geoff named the dog Jasmine (sounds like JAZZ-men). She was a greyhound. In some places, greyhounds are bred to race on a track. Dog racing is a popular sport. But when a dog starts to lose races, some heartless dog owners don't want to feed or care for them anymore. Geoff thinks that may be what happened to Jasmine.

Geoff and his co-workers nursed Jasmine back to health. They also tried to win her trust. Sudden movements and loud noises scared her. So everyone moved slowly. They tried to talk quietly. In time, Jasmine learned to trust them. After several weeks of special care and good food, she grew healthy and happy.

Geoff started to look for someone to adopt Jasmine. He wanted to find a nice family to love her and take care of her.

In the meantime, Jasmine found her own place. It was on the couch in the sanctuary office.

Every time someone brought in a box or a cage, Jasmine looked up. Then she unfolded her long legs and stepped down from the couch. She poked her long nose inside the box. She sniffed at whatever animal had been brought in for help. Then she gave it a gentle lick. Geoff thought Jasmine was telling the animals, "Don't worry. You're safe now."

Jasmine licked fox and badger cubs. She licked rabbits. "She even let the birds perch on the bridge of her nose," Geoff says.

Soon Jasmine became the official greeter at the sanctuary. "She seemed to have a need to comfort every creature, great and small," Geoff recalls. So many helpless animals needed a friend like Jasmine! She welcomed owls, swans, hedgehogs, and many others to the sanctuary. After a while, Geoff decided the sanctuary needed Jasmine. So he adopted her.

One day, Geoff got a call from the local train station. Two newborn puppies had been found on the tracks. Could Geoff come and get them?

Geoff jumped into his car. On the way back with the puppies, he wondered what Jasmine would do. He knew she had never

Dogs communicate with each other by scent, body position, the expressions on their faces, and the sounds they make.

had puppies of her own. Would she know how to help these newborns?

As soon as Geoff brought the puppies in, Jasmine leaped off the couch. With her mouth, she picked one puppy up by the scruff of his neck. She carried him to the couch. She went back for the other pup. Then she jumped onto the couch herself. She tucked those babies close to her tummy and curled around them. Somehow, she knew they needed more than a lick.

When Geoff came back with bottles of warm goat's milk, Jasmine nudged the puppies awake. After feeding them, Geoff returned the pups to Jasmine. She licked them clean and settled them in for another nap. *That went well,* thought Geoff. He smiled at Jasmine and the puppies.

Built for Speed

Greyhounds are one of the oldest dog breeds. Ancient Egyptians hunted with them nearly 3,000 years ago. Tomb carvings show the dogs chasing deer and mountain goats. They were brought to England more than 1,000 years ago. Greyhounds are the second fastest land animals. Only cheetahs are swifter. With their long legs and lean bodies, greyhounds can run like the wind. In races, they have been clocked at 45 miles (72 km) an hour!

Bramble looks lively here, but the fawn was very sick when he first came to the animal sanctuary.

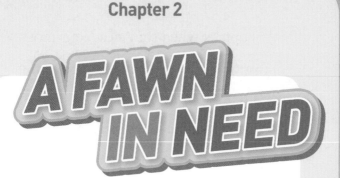

A FAWN IN NEED

Geoff named the puppies Buster and Toby. Both of them were terriers (sounds like TER-ee-ers). And both did just fine, thanks to Jasmine. Geoff thinks she might have saved their lives.

That's because Jasmine was more than just a good friend to Buster and Toby. By keeping them safe and warm with her body, she also acted like a mother dog to the little puppies when they needed it most.

Another time someone dropped off a very small, very weak fox cub at the sanctuary. Jasmine knew what a mom would do. With Geoff and Jasmine's help, the fox cub grew lively and strong. Geoff named her Roxy. Roxy and Jasmine became great friends. They liked going on walks together.

Soon another animal needed Jasmine's special touch. It was a tiny baby deer, or fawn. Two people hiking through the woods found it lying out in the open. It was right next to the path. Normally, mother deer keep their babies hidden. The hikers could tell right away that this fawn was in trouble. At first they wondered, *Is it even breathing?* Then they saw it was alive. But they knew it couldn't survive by itself.

The hikers lifted the fawn and carried him to their car. They took him to a veterinarian (sounds like vet-er-ih-NARE-ee-en). The vet thought the fawn was about two weeks old. He also thought there was no hope for it. "He's too far gone," the vet said. "He can't be saved." But the people who found him wouldn't give up.

They drove on until they reached the wildlife sanctuary. "Can you help, please?" they asked Stacey Clarke. Stacey works at the sanctuary with Geoff. The people told Stacey the vet thought the fawn would die. Stacey didn't say so, but she agreed with the vet. The fawn had been alone and without food for far too long. But she agreed to try.

In the end, however, it was Jasmine who kept the fawn alive.

She had a little help from Geoff and Stacey, of course. They fed the fawn bottles of warm goat's milk every three to four hours. Then Jasmine took over. She seemed to sense that the fawn not only needed a friend. He also needed some mothering. Jasmine was just the dog to give it to him. She licked and cleaned the fawn. She snuggled with him on the couch and kept him warm. Day by day, the fawn grew stronger. Finally, he was out of danger. When Geoff was sure that the fawn was going to make it, he named him Bramble.

When Bramble grew strong enough, he and Jasmine went for walks together. Sometimes a chipmunk surprised them, or a loud bird cried nearby. Then Bramble hid underneath Jasmine.

Bramble stuck to Jasmine like glue. "Bramble walked between her legs and they kept kissing each other," Geoff recalls. "They walked together round the sanctuary. It was a real treat to see them."

Bramble often checked with Jasmine by putting his nose to her nose. Deer have an excellent sense of smell. In the wild, Bramble would have touched noses with his mother often during the day. He would have learned, by the way his mother's nose smelled, if a

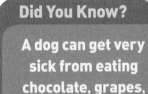

Did You Know?

A dog can get very sick from eating chocolate, grapes, or raisins.

place or another animal was safe. He might have been trying this with Jasmine.

Fast Friends

Greyhounds only race until they are three or four years old. Then they retire from the track. Many groups try to find forever homes for former race dogs. One of them, called Adopt-A-Greyhound, says, "We'd like to introduce you to the fastest friend you'll ever meet!"

Adopt-A-Greyhound helps people turn racing dogs into pets. Life in a house is different than life at the racetrack. For example, the dogs need to be taught how to walk up and down stairs. That's something they never had to do when they were racers.

Seeing Bramble and Jasmine together surprised visitors. Why would a dog and a deer become such good friends? It had a lot to do with Bramble's age. Scientists say very young animals are up for anything. They don't know if something is weird. Their motto seems to be, "If it feels good, do it!"

Also, living at the sanctuary makes odd friendships possible. After all, none of the animals has to worry about food. They know that Geoff and Stacey will feed them. In the wild, a hungry fox might gobble up a duckling. In the sanctuary, the rattle of plastic dishes filled with kibble and meat is what makes them hungry, not their little duck friend.

Jasmine and Bramble were lucky to have found each other.

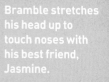

Bramble stretches his head up to touch noses with his best friend, Jasmine.

Chapter 3

ONE OF A KIND

Geoff thinks there could be another reason for Jasmine and Bramble's strong friendship. They kind of looked alike. They both had long legs. They both had pointy faces with long noses. They both had big brown eyes and small delicate ears. They even had the same fur color. Bramble might have thought, *Are you my mother?*

It wasn't long before Bramble grew too big to snuggle with Jasmine on the couch. Soon he was old enough to release into the wild. But there was a problem. Bramble had been at the sanctuary for several months. That was long enough for him to think of Geoff and Stacey as his friends. In the woods, he wouldn't last long if he thought every person he met was his friend.

Geoff also thought that separating Jasmine and Bramble would be mean. The greyhound and deer didn't spend all their time together anymore. But when Jasmine came out of the office, she always looked for Bramble. They still loved to walk together. Bramble might run off to check out a noise, but he always came back to Jasmine's side. They rubbed their cheeks together. They leaned on each other. They were such good friends.

So Bramble ended up staying. Jasmine continued to welcome new animals in the office. Bramble also made some new friends. He met a badger named Humbug. He hung out with a big buzzard named Ellie. He took walks with Roxy the fox.

Did You Know?

When a roe deer is scared, it makes a barking sound.

Bramble really hit it off with a turkey named Tinsel. Nobody knows how the two animals got together. It could be that Bramble just liked what was in Tinsel's dinner bowl. Maybe he decided to stick around for more.

Now, Bramble curls up in the barn to sleep with Tinsel every night. Tinsel pecks at Bramble's face. When he gobbles, Bramble comes around to see what's up.

Jasmine used to visit Bramble and Tinsel in the barn. She would lick Bramble's face and stay with them for a while. Jasmine's life at the sanctuary was very happy. She loved everybody, and they loved her. So it was sad when she passed away from old age in 2011. Geoff isn't sure exactly how old Jasmine was. He does know that she made the world a better place, one animal orphan at a time. Today her spot on the couch is sometimes taken by a new puppy or fox cub. But there will never be another Jasmine, Geoff says. The gentle greyhound was one of a kind. Jasmine was a best friend to all.

Deer Details

Deer live on every continent except Antarctica. They make their home in woodlands, forests, and mountains. They are also found in deserts and grasslands. There are more than 43 different kinds of deer.

Bramble is a roe deer. Roe deer live in England and other parts of Europe. In North America, most deer are white-tailed deer. Roe deer are about half as big as white-tailed deer. Roe deer and white-tailed deer both have reddish fur in the summer. In winter their fur turns gray.

Owen the hippo follows Mzee the tortoise wherever he goes.

OWEN AND MZEE: ODD COUPLE

Owen is about one year old in this picture. At the time, the cute little hippo weighed about 600 pounds (272 kg).

Little Lost HIPPO

December 2003, Malindi, Kenya

n Christmas Day the beach in Malindi (sounds like ma-LIN-dee), Kenya, was crowded. Usually people on a beach watch the waves. Not today on this beach! Everybody was looking at a group of hippopotamuses, or hippos.

The hippos had appeared on the beach a few days earlier. Before that, they had lived in a river many miles away. Then heavy rains came and flooded the river. The fast-moving water washed the hippos downstream. They ended up at the beach.

The Malindi beach is popular with tourists. The white sand and turquoise-blue ocean are two reasons why people want to go to there. A third reason is that you can see a lot of fantastic animals nearby. Kenya, a country on the east coast of Africa, is home to elephants, eagles, giraffes, zebras, and more.

The tourists probably thought it was exciting to have the hippos on the beach. The villagers knew better. Even from a distance, the adult hippos looked big and strong. There was a calf, or baby, too. The adults would try to protect it. Hippos can be dangerous to people. And the ocean can be dangerous for hippos. They can't swim in the ocean.

That night many people went to bed thinking about the hippos. By morning, there was something else to worry about.

Early in the morning on December 26, 2004, an underwater earthquake exploded in the Indian Ocean. It was the third strongest earthquake in history. It triggered a series of massive waves. The giant waves wiped out beaches and towns in Indonesia. Many people were hurt or killed. That evening, the waves hit the coast of Kenya. They weren't as big by then, but they were still big enough to cause damage.

River Horses

Hippopotamus means "river horse" in ancient Greek. Hippos live in Africa. The sun there is strong and hot. Water keeps the hippos cool. Being underwater protects them from sunburn. They even nap in the water. They lift their noses out just enough to get a breath, but not enough to wake themselves up!

Hippos can't really swim. Their bodies are too heavy. They move through the water by sinking to the river bottom. Then they push off with their legs.

The next day, people came out to see the Malindi beach. Boats had been thrown up on the shore. Beach chairs were bobbing in the ocean. And the hippos? There was only one left—the calf. People did not know what happened to the others. One thing was certain. The calf needed to be rescued.

First, they needed to catch it. Fishermen unrolled their big nets. Moving in a line, they held the nets in front of them. They inched toward the hippo. Villagers and tourists helped. But hippos are fast. They're slippery, too, and big. This little baby weighed about 600 pounds (272 kg)! Again and again the people chased him. No luck. When they zigged, he zagged.

The hippo calf ran back and forth on the reef for hours. Finally, the rescuers trapped him in a net. Everyone cheered! But then the calf kicked and twisted. He broke the net that held him. He got loose again. The rescuers were exhausted, but they were determined. They traded their fishing nets for shark nets. Shark nets are much stronger.

Finally, a visitor named Owen Sobien tackled the hippo. Owen played rugby at home in France, so he knew how to tackle! Everyone quickly threw their nets over the hippo. They pinned him down. Caught! Hundreds of people cheered. They clapped and whistled. What a relief! Someone thought to call the nearest wildlife sanctuary, Haller Park. It's near Mombasa (sounds like mom-BAH-sah), a town about 50 miles (80 km) down the coast.

Dr. Paula Kahumbu (ka-HUM-boo) was the manager at Haller Park. She knew that if they didn't go get the hippo, he had no chance at all. She asked Stephen Tuei (too-WAY) to go with her. He is the chief animal caretaker at Haller Park.

Paula and Stephen jumped in her truck. When they got to Malindi, they saw the calf. He was tied up, lying on his side in the back of a truck. The hippo was breathing hard. He had cuts and scratches from the reef. He had a sunburn. But he was alive.

Paula asked the rescuers if they had named the hippo calf. They hadn't yet. People called out ideas. Finally, everyone started yelling, "Owen! Owen!" They named the hippo after the brave man who tackled him.

Owen wants to play, so he nudges Mzee to wake him. Mzee moves on turtle time— slow and steady.

Chapter 2

A NEW FRIEND

The people in Malindi helped Paula and Stephen move Owen into Paula's truck. Then Paula and Stephen drove back to Haller Park. On the way, they talked about what to do with Owen.

Haller Park already had a few adult hippos. They lived in a fenced-in area, or enclosure (sounds like en-KLO-zhur), with antelopes and other big animals. Owen couldn't live with them. Grown hippos might kick and bite babies they're not related to. The best place for Owen would be with the smaller, gentler animals. They would put him in an enclosure with some monkeys and a few slow-moving tortoises.

At the park, Paula backed the truck up to the enclosure. She and Stephen peeled the nets off Owen. Then they stood back. Owen struggled to his feet. He ran away from the scary people. He ran straight to a giant tortoise and hid behind him. That sure surprised the tortoise!

The tortoise was named Mzee (sounds like mah-ZAY). He was about 130 years old. Owen was about one year old.

Mzee was known for being a bit grumpy. He scooted away from Owen, but Owen stayed close to him. Paula and Stephen left for the night. They never dreamed what they'd see in the morning.

The next day Owen was still peeking out from behind Mzee. But guess what? Mzee wasn't moving away. He even seemed to like the little guy. As for Owen, he saw Mzee was round like a hippo. He was gray like a hippo. Did Owen think Mzee was a hippo? No one knows, but scientists think Mzee's shape and color might have been comforting to Owen.

Hippos in the wild live together in family groups. Owen must have felt very lonely without his hippo family. He was badly in need of a friend.

Over the next few days, it became clear that Mzee was the friend Owen needed. Owen was still very weak. He didn't seem to know what to eat. Stephen added special animal food called dairy cubes to the cabbage, grasses, and carrots he left for Owen and Mzee. When Mzee started to eat a dairy cube, so did Owen. He was copying Mzee!

Owen watched Mzee constantly. He started eating the grasses Mzee ate. He munched the same leaves. It was like Mzee was teaching him what to eat.

In the wild, reptiles like Mzee do not make friends with mammals like Owen. They don't really make friends at all. But over the next few months, Mzee amazed everyone at the sanctuary. The tortoise seemed really fond of the growing hippo.

Old-Timers

Mzee is an Aldabra (sounds like all-DAH-bruh) tortoise. The Aldabra tortoise is one of the longest-living land animals on Earth.

One of the oldest Aldabra tortoises known to scientists died in 2006. It was 250 years old! That tortoise was alive back when pirates roamed the oceans. Pirates and sailors often kept tortoises and sea turtles on their ships. They weren't pets—they were food. The sailors kept them on their backs so they couldn't run away.

Today, Mzee is about 140 years old. He could live another 100 years or more!

Mzee rested his head on Owen's stomach. He waited for him when they took walks. When they rested, they were always touching each other.

Sometimes Owen nipped at Mzee's back legs. If he wanted his friend to turn left, he'd nip at his left leg. Nip right, turn right. Mzee was happy to go along with this. He gave Owen a few nips of his own. Sometimes if Owen got too slow on a walk, Mzee stretched his neck and nipped Owen's tail. That sure got Owen's attention!

Owen also liked to lick Mzee's head. That was OK. Then he started putting his huge mouth around his Mzee's little head. *That* was a bit much. It made the caretakers pay attention.

Another hippo had hurt Mzee by accident before Owen arrived at the park. That hippo had rolled Mzee like a ball, cracking the top of Mzee's shell. Stephen and Paula called other scientists and vets for advice. They were worried Owen might accidentally hurt Mzee. They were also worried about Owen.

Owen was not acting like a hippo anymore. He was acting like a tortoise! Hippos spend their days in the water. But Owen wanted to be with Mzee. When he should have been napping, he was taking a long, slow walk with Mzee. At night, Owen should have been eating a big dinner. Instead, he ate what Mzee ate.

Paula and Stephen and the other scientists agreed that Owen needed to learn how to be a hippo.

A hippo sniffs a tasty treat. In the wild, hippos can eat more than 80 pounds (35 kg) of grass a day!

Chapter 3

HAPPY HIPPOS

Paula and Stephen decided to build a new enclosure for Owen. They designed one with a waterfall and an island. It had ponds ringed with trees and plants that hippos like to eat. When it was finished, they moved a hippo named Cleo into it first.

Everyone at Haller Park loved Cleo. She liked to balance sticks on her nose. Maybe Cleo and Owen could be friends. Maybe she could teach him to act like a hippo.

Cleo loved the new space. She trotted around it. She swam in every pool.

In December 2006, Stephen and Paula got ready to move Owen into the new space. They piled dairy cubes and bananas at the far side of a sturdy moving box. As they hoped, Owen wandered into the big box to check out the food. They shut the door behind him.

The caretakers lifted the box onto a truck. They drove it to the new enclosure. But before they let Owen out, they moved his pal Mzee to the new space, too. They hoped he would make Owen feel more comfortable in his new home.

When they let Owen out, he ran into

the woods and hid. Mzee went to get him. The two of them walked around the area.

Then Owen heard Cleo. She honked from the pond. Owen was curious but afraid. Smart boy. Cleo was twice his size and more than twice his age. She could do some damage. She was not related to Owen. She might have seen him as a threat.

Did You Know?

Male Aldabra tortoises weigh about 400 pounds (181 kg). Females weigh about 300 pounds (136 kg).

For the next few days, Cleo chased Owen. Owen ran and hid. Stephen and Paula kept their fingers crossed. They started to think it wasn't going to work. Then one day they found Cleo and Owen in the pond together.

A Shape to Love

When Owen met Mzee, a man named Peter Greste took a photograph. It was a picture of Owen with his head resting on Mzee's foot. Everyone who saw it fell in love with Owen and Mzee. Dr. Paula helped write a book about the two friends. Lots of kids read the book.

One day, a student in Canada showed her teacher one of the photos in the book. To her, the back of Mzee's shell looked exactly like a hippo face. Maybe that's what Owen saw and liked so much. What do you think?

Cleo popped her head out of the water as Owen dove down head first. Stephen and Paula could see his little tail wagging madly. It made them laugh.

Owen and Cleo started spending more time together. They played a game Stephen called Skipping Hippos. In the pond, Cleo would bounce away from Owen. He bounced after her. When he got close to her, he'd turn and bounce away. Then she bounced back after him. Cleo taught Owen that he could sleep underwater. She also taught him new sounds like honking and bellowing: hippo sounds!

In March 2007, the Haller staff moved Mzee back to his old home. Owen was spending less time with Mzee and more time with Cleo. And Cleo was a little rough with Mzee. Stephen worried about Mzee's safety.

People are sad that Owen and Mzee aren't together anymore. But it's not sad for them. Cleo and Owen are very happy together. Maybe they'll have hippo babies one day. Mzee seems happy, too. There are a few new tortoises in his enclosure. Imagine what Mzee might say if he could tell his new friends about Owen!

THE END

DON'T MISS!

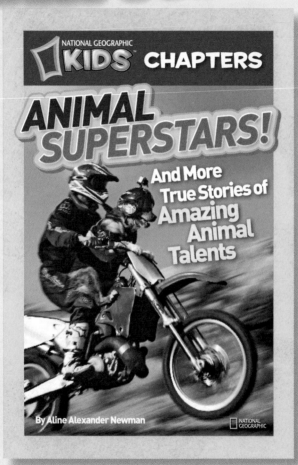

NATIONAL GEOGRAPHIC **KIDS** CHAPTERS

ANIMAL SUPERSTARS!

And More True Stories of Amazing Animal Talents

By Aline Alexander Newman

NATIONAL GEOGRAPHIC

Turn the page for a sneak preview . . .

Ready to ride, Opee pants with excitement. His helmet has a camera on top.

Chapter 1

EASY RIDER

April 2006, San Diego, California

Opee the Australian (sounds like AH-STRALE-YAN) shepherd cocks his head and listens. Has Mike entered the garage? The devoted dog jumps to his feet and runs toward the sound. Barking excitedly, he leaps onto the gas tank of Mike Schelin's dirt bike. Opee's pink tongue hangs out. His front paws rest on the handlebars.

Mike grins. He slips a helmet and goggles on the happy dog's head. He hops on the bike behind Opee and kicks the starter with his heel. Off they go across the California desert.

Mike is a professional motocross (sounds like MOE-TOE-CROSS) racer. And so is Opee! Motocross is a form of cross-country motorcycle racing. Racers ride special motocross bikes, also called dirt bikes. They race on rugged tracks that are closed to normal traffic.

Mike and Opee's story started when Mike Schelin was 35 years old. Things had not been going well for him lately and he was unhappy. *Cheer up!* he told himself. But he didn't know how. So he sat down with a pad and pencil.

He made a list of all the things that made him feel good.

Later Mike read what he wrote. *Hmm,* he thought, *dogs are first on my list. I need a job that lets me bring a dog to work.*

Soon Mike quit his job selling computers and moved to San Diego, California. He met a man there who let Mike live in an old house for free. In return, Mike agreed to fix up the place. But something was missing. Mike needed a dog to keep him company.

He called a woman who had an Australian shepherd puppy for sale. They agreed to meet on a country road where 75 mailboxes stood in a row.

Mike spotted the mailboxes first. Then he saw a mother dog and puppy playing in the grass. The puppy had soft, floppy ears. His furry coat had patches of black, brown, and gray with white around his neck. His eyes were different colors. One was blue and the other was brown. Mike scooped him up, and slurp! The little furball stuck out his tongue and licked Mike's face. Mike paid the woman and drove home with the puppy.

Mike didn't think of the dog as a pet. He thought of him more as a friend, or even a brother. He named the pup Opee, his own nickname as a child.

The next day, Mike woke up to whining. "Are you hungry, fella?" Mike asked. He poured some kibble into a plastic bowl and fixed himself a cup of coffee.

Feeling Upset?

Get a pup. Dogs understand when people are nervous or scared. Seeing you cry makes a dog feel bad. It will tuck its tail and bow its head, say scientists at the University of London, in England. A dog will snuggle against you and give you a doggie hug. You can bury your face in its soft fur and it will lick your cheek.

Pretty soon, you will stop thinking about yourself and think about your pup instead. You might even smile.

The house was a mess. A table saw stood in the middle of the living room. Rows of bare wooden studs rose like jail bars at one end of the room. Piles of sweet-smelling sawdust littered the floor.

Mike grabbed a hammer and started to work. Opee followed behind, leaving paw prints in the dust. Later he curled up in Mike's toolbox to sleep.

One day, Mike and Opee drove to the hardware store for supplies. When they got there, Mike set the puppy on a flatbed cart. "Stay," he said. Opee did. Mike was surprised by how well he obeyed. "He just seemed to get it," Mike said.

On weekends, Mike relaxed by riding his dirt bike in the desert. He took Opee with him. Mike thought Opee would enjoy running off-leash. Maybe he'd run after lizards and snakes. But Opee chased Mike instead. He chased him uphill and downhill. Over bumps and pits and in clouds of dust. The dog never stopped.

Mike decided to buy a quad—a four-wheeled off-road motorbike with a seat big enough for two. Now Opee could ride along! But how to keep the dust out of Opee's eyes? Mike had an idea. First he cut a slit in the middle of a sock. Then he slipped a pair of goggles through the slit and tied the ends of the sock under Opee's chin. Perfect!

Want to know what happens next? Be sure to check out *Animal Superstars!* Available wherever books and ebooks are sold.

INDEX

MORE INFORMATION

To find more information about the animal species in this book and other unusual friendships, check out these books and websites:

Face to Face With Orangutans,
by Tim Laman and Cheryl Knott, National Geographic, 2009

125 True Stories of Amazing Animals,
National Geographic, 2012

Koko's Kids Club
www.koko.org/kidsclub

San Diego Zoo "Animal Bytes: Hippopotamus"
www.sandiegozoo.org/animalbytes/t-hippopotamus.html

San Francisco Zoo "Animals: Western Lowland Gorilla"
www.sfzoo.org/westernlowlandgorilla

Unlikely Friendships
http://unlikelyfriendshipsbook.tumblr.com

This book is dedicated to my BFF, Pat Normandeau
—A.S.

CREDITS

Thanks to National Geographic Channel for the photos of Roscoe and Suryia, as seen on Nat Geo WILD's *Unlikely Animal Friends*.

Cover, Stevi Calandra/National Geographic Channels; 4-5, Stevi Calandra/National Geographic Channels; 6, MyrtleBeachSafari.com/Barry Bland; 11 (up, right), Stephaniellen/Shutterstock; 14, MyrtleBeachSafari.com/Barry Bland; 21 (up), Rhett A. Butler/mongabay.com; 22, MyrtleBeachSafari.com/Barry Bland; 26 (up), © Ardiles Rante/Barcroft Media; 28-29, Ron Cohn/Gorilla Foundation/koko.org; 30, Ron Cohn/Gorilla Foundation/koko.org; 34, Ronald Cohn/National Geographic Stock; 36, Ron Cohn/Gorilla Foundation/koko.org; 43, Stuart Key/Dreamstime.com; 44, Ron Cohn/Gorilla Foundation/koko.org; 50, Ron Cohn/Gorilla Foundation/koko.org; 52-53, Caters News Agency; 54, Nuneaton and Warwickshire Wildlife Sanctuary; 61, Utekhina Anna/Shutterstock; 62, Nuneaton and Warwickshire Wildlife Sanctuary; 68, EcoPrint/Shutterstock; 70 (Background), Andrei Calangiu/Dreamstime.com; 70, Nuneaton and Warwickshire Wildlife Sanctuary; 75, Erik Mandre/Dreamstime.com; 76-77, Reuters/Antony Njuguna; 78, Associated Press; 82, Karin Van Ijzendoorn/Dreamstime.com; 86, Associated Press; 91, Daniel Wilson/Shutterstock; 94, Rgbe/Dreamstime.com; 98, Reuters/Antony Njuguna; 101, AP Images/Chris Carlson; 102, AP Images/Chris Carlson; 107, Joyce Marrero/Shutterstock; 111, MyrtleBeachSafari.com/Barry Bland.

ACKNOWLEDGMENTS

Amy Shields thanks the following organizations for helping to make this book possible:

The Gorilla Foundation
www.koko.org

Nuneaton & Warwickshire Wildlife Sanctuary
www.nuneatonwildlife.co.uk

Owen & Mzee
www.owenandmzee.com

T.I.G.E.R.S.
www.suryiaandroscoe.com